PIANO · VOCAL · GUITAR

twilight

D0473940

Due to licensing restrictions, "Flightless Bird, American Mouth" is not included in this folio.

SUMMIT ENTERTAINMENT PRESENTS "TWILIGHT"

A TEMPLE HILL PRODUCTION IN ASSOCIATION WITH MAVERICK FILMS KRISTEN STEWART ROBERT PATTINSON BILLY BURKE PETER FACINELLI

CASTING BY TRICIA WOOD, CSA DEBORAH AQUILA, CSA MUSIC BY CARTER BURWELL MUSIC SUPERVISOR ALEXANDRA PATSAVAS COSTUME DESIGNER WENDY CHUCK EDITOR NANCY RICHARDSON, A.C.E. DIRECTOR OF PHOTOGRAPHY ELIOTT DAVIS

EXECUTIVE PRODUCERS KAREN ROSENFELT MARTY BOWEN GUY OSEARY MICHELE IMPERATO STABILE PRODUCED BY MARK MORGAN GREG MOORADIAN WYCK GODFREY

PG-13 PARENTS STRONGLY CAUTIONED Some Material May Be Inappropriate for Children Under 13 Some Violence and a Scene of Sensuality. BASED ON THE NOVEL "TWILIGHT" BY STEPHENIE MEYER SCREENPLAY BY MELISSA ROSENBERG DIRECTED BY CATHERINE HARDWICKE

Original Motion Film Soundtrack Available on Atlantic Records TWILIGHTTHEMOVIE.COM © 2008 SUMMIT ENTERTAINMENT LLC. ALL RIGHTS RESERVED.

ISBN 978-1-4234-6884-4

HAL•LEONARD® CORPORATION

7777 W. BLUEMOUND RD. P.O. BOX 13819 MILWAUKEE, WI 53213

For all works contained herein:
Unauthorized copying, arranging, adapting, recording or public performance is an infringement of copyright.
Infringers are liable under the law.

Visit Hal Leonard Online at
www.halleonard.com

james

twilight

SUPERMASSIVE BLACK HOLE

Words and Music by
MATTHEW BELLAMY

Alternative Rock

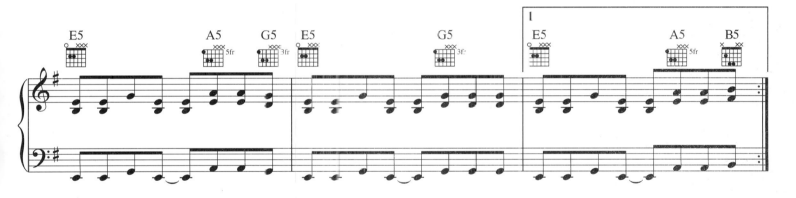

Oh, __ ba - by, don't you know __ I suf - fer? __
I __ thought I was a fool __ for no __ one. __

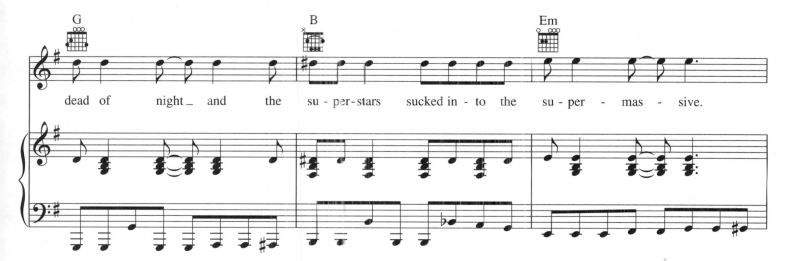

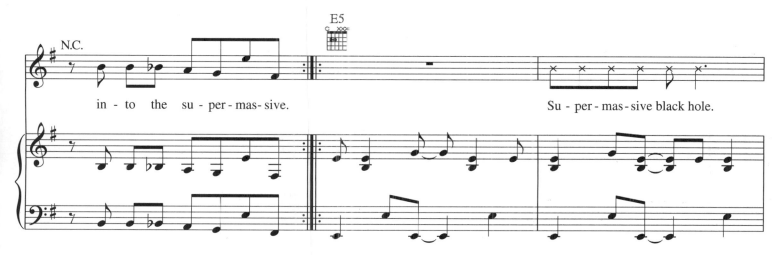

DECODE

Words and Music by TAYLOR YORK,
HAYLEY WILLIAMS and JOSH FARRO

Moderate Rock

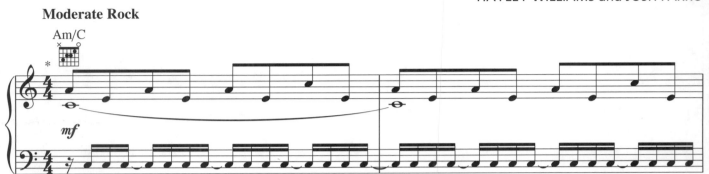

How can I de-cide what's right when you're cloud-ing up my mind?
The truth is hid-ing in your eyes and it's hang-ing on your tongue,

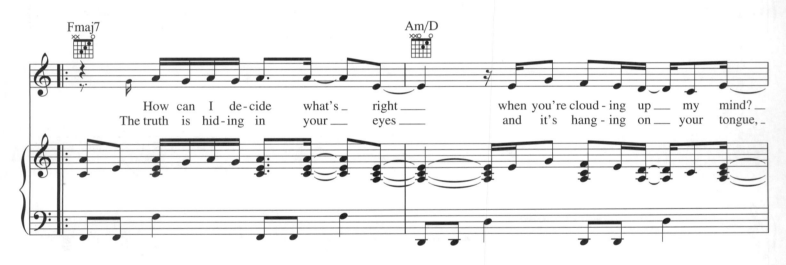

I can't win, you're los-ing fight all the time.
just boil-ing in my blood. But you think that I can't see

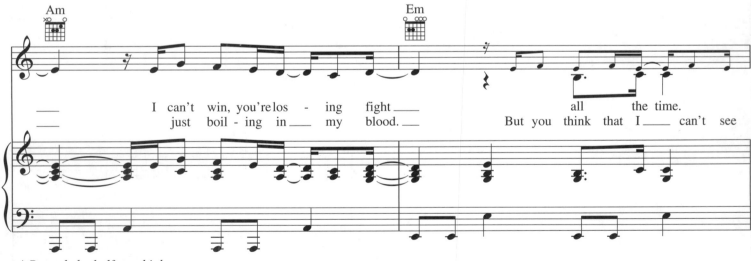

* Recorded a half step higher.

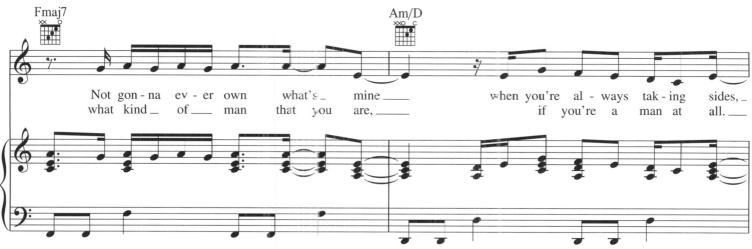

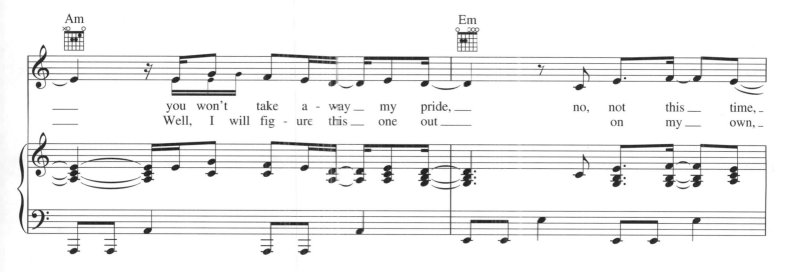

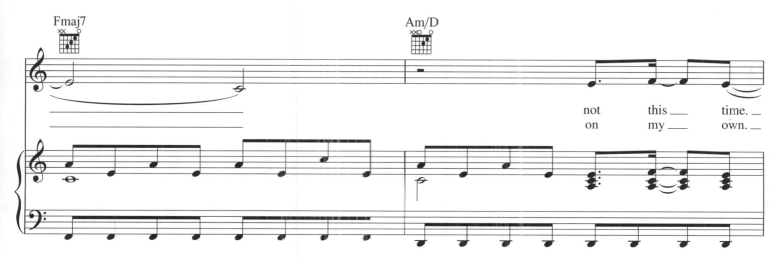

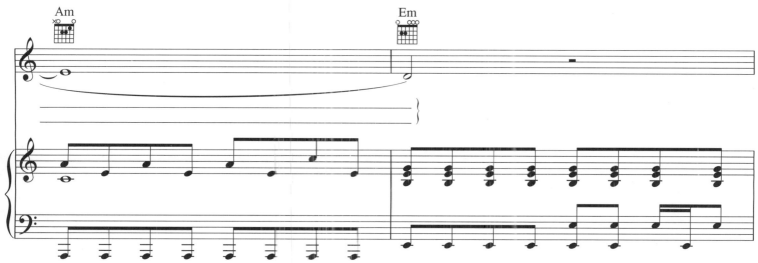

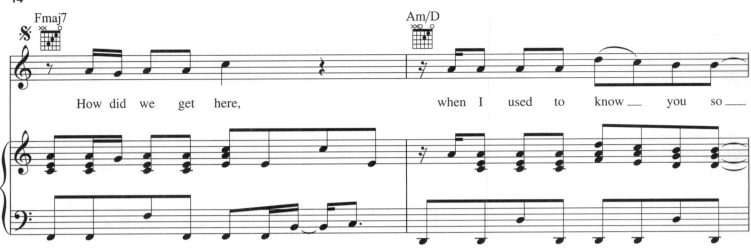

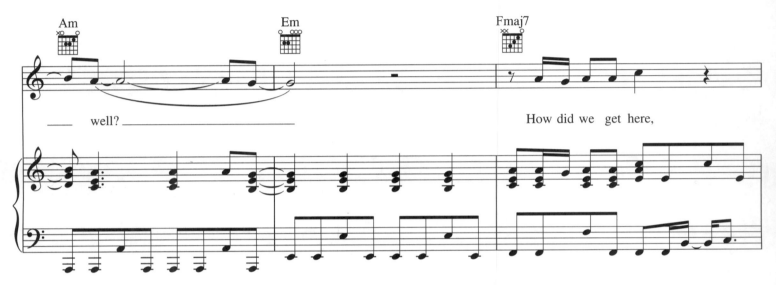

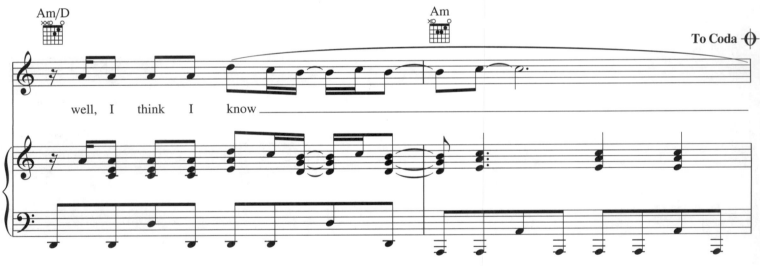

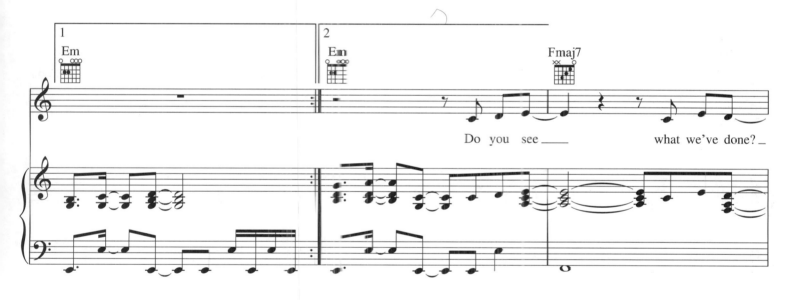

see   what we've done? ___   we've gone and made such   fools   of our -

selves.   Yeah. _____

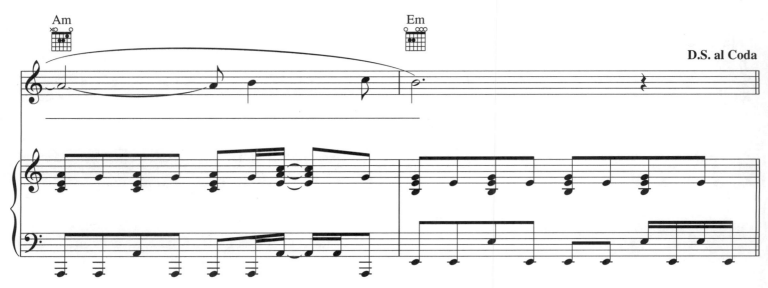

D.S. al Coda

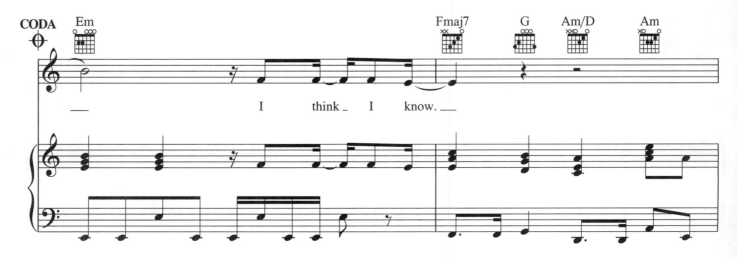

I   think _ I   know. __

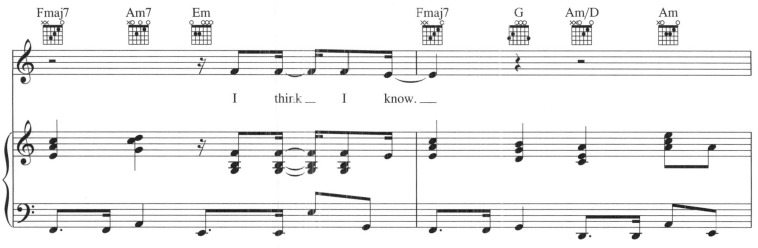

I think __ I know. __

There is ___ some - thing

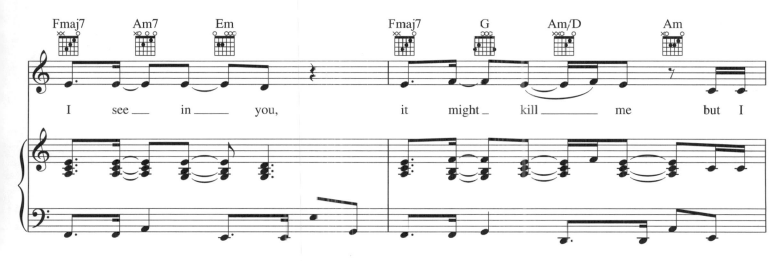

I see __ in ___ you, it might __ kill ___ me but I

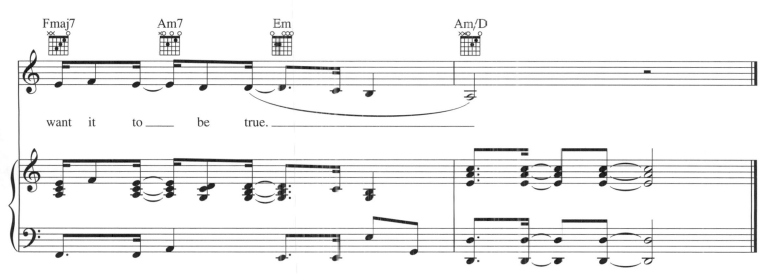

want it to ___ be true. ___

FULL MOON

Words and Music by THEO KEATING
and SIMON LORD

Folky Electronica

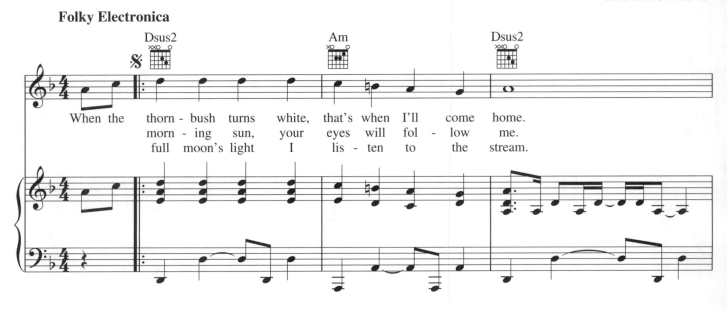

When the thorn-bush turns white, that's when I'll come home.
morn-ing sun, your eyes will fol-low me.
full moon's light I lis-ten to the stream.

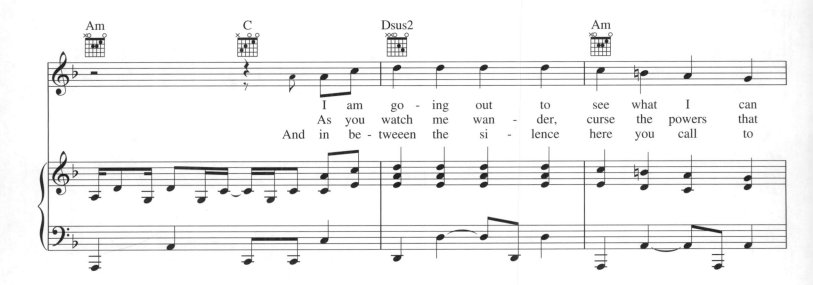

I am go-ing out to see what I can
As you watch me wan-der, curse the powers that
And in be-tween the si-lence here you call to

sow.
be.
me.

And I don't know where I'll
'Cause all I want is here and
But if I don't know where I

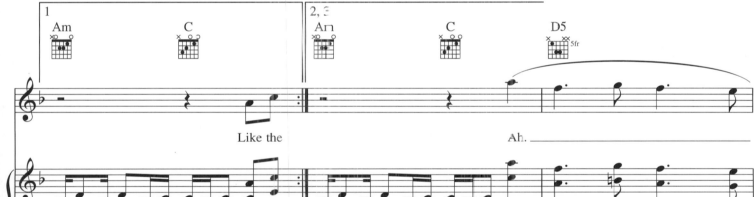

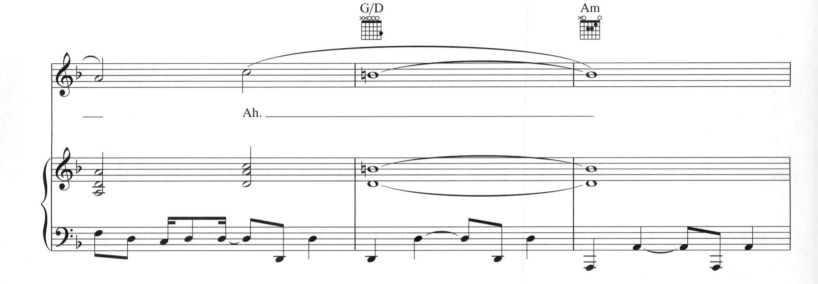

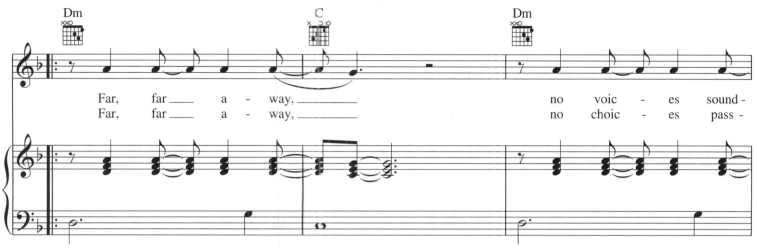

Far, far ___ a - way, _____ no voic - es sound-
Far, far ___ a - way, _____ no choic - es pass-

- ing, no one ___ a - round ___ me
- ing, no time ___ con - founds ___ me

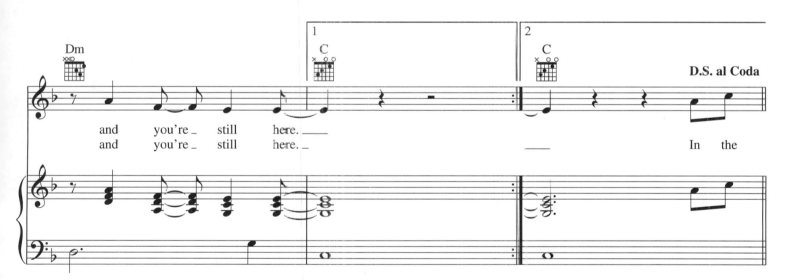

and you're _ still here. ___
and you're _ still here. _ In the

D.S. al Coda

CODA

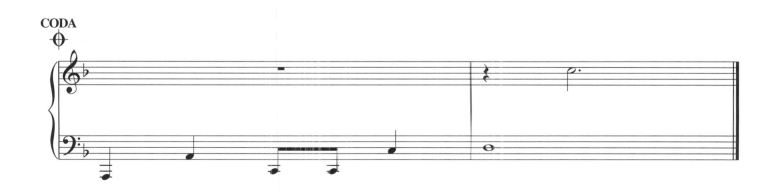

LEAVE OUT ALL THE REST

Words and Music by MIKE SHINODA,
JOE HAHN, BRAD DELSON, ROB BOURDON,
CHESTER BENNINGTON and DAVE FARRELL

Slow Rock

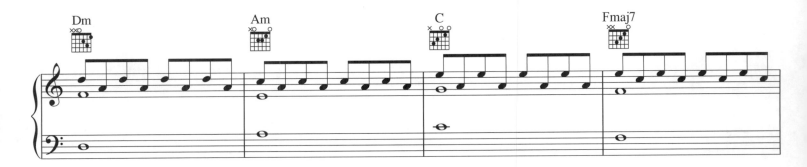

I dreamed _ I was miss-ing, you _ were so scared but no _ one would
fraid, I've tak - en my

lis - ten 'cause no _ one else cared. Af - ter my
beat - ing, I've shed _ but I'm me. I'm strong _ on the

sent me, and when you're feel - ing emp - ty keep me in your mem-

-'ry, leave out all the rest, ___ leave out all the rest. ___ Don't be a -

For - get - ting all the hurt in - side, you've learned ___ to hide ___ so well. ___

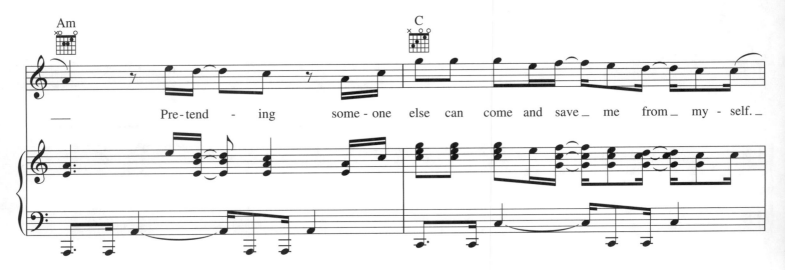

___ Pre - tend - ing some - one else can come and save ___ me from ___ my - self. ___

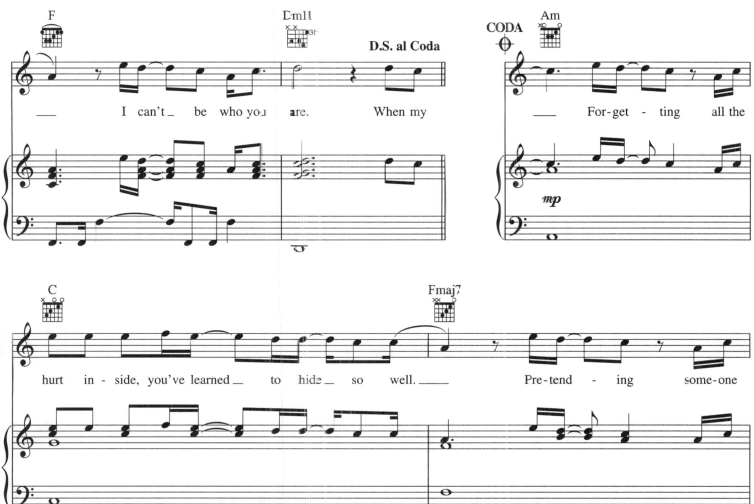

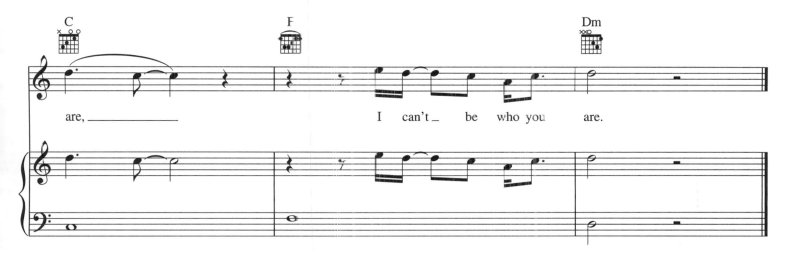

SPOTLIGHT
(Twilight Remix)

Words and Music by
PAUL MEANY

Ah.

Ah.

You got a whole lot left to say ___ now.

You knocked all your

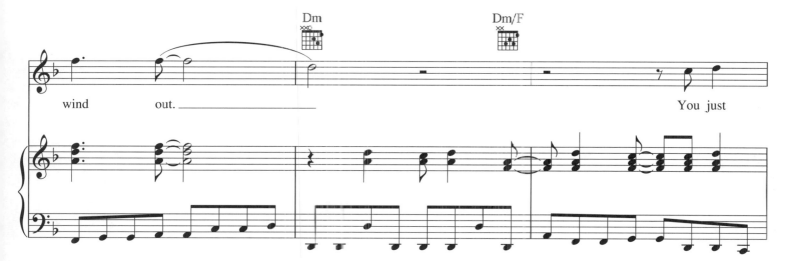

wind out. _____ You just

tried too hard and you __ froze. _____

I _____ know, I _____

28

know.   What do you say?

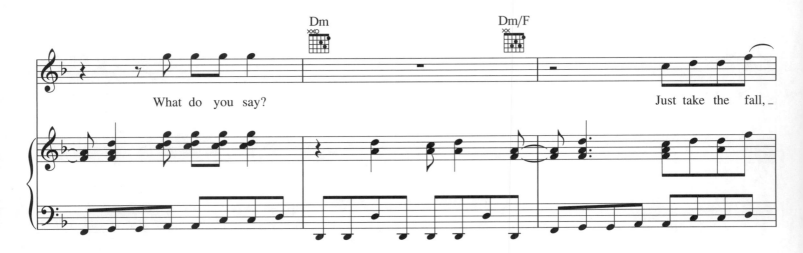

What do you say?   Just take the fall,

you're one ___ of us.

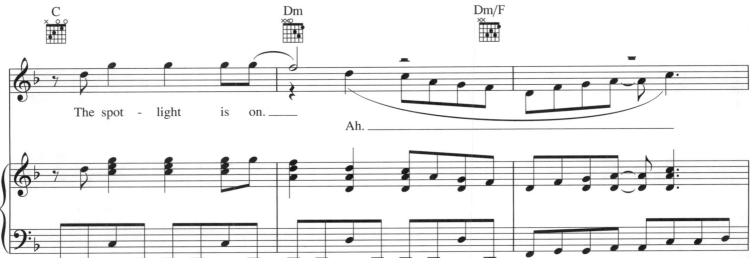

The spot - light is on. ___   Ah. ___

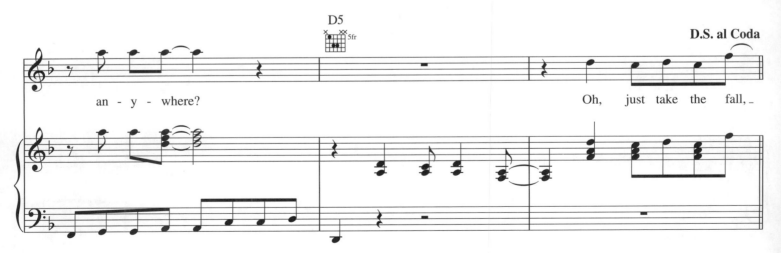

CODA

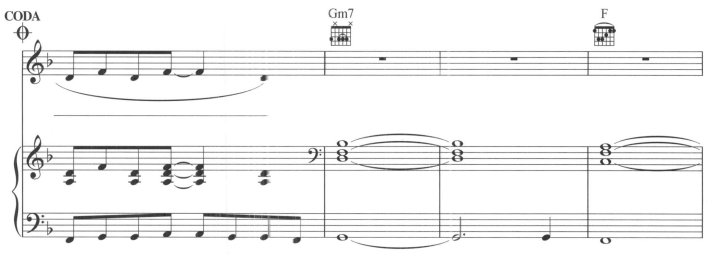

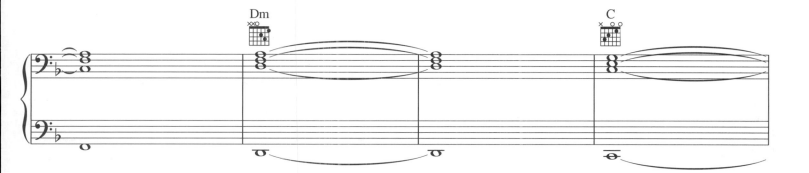

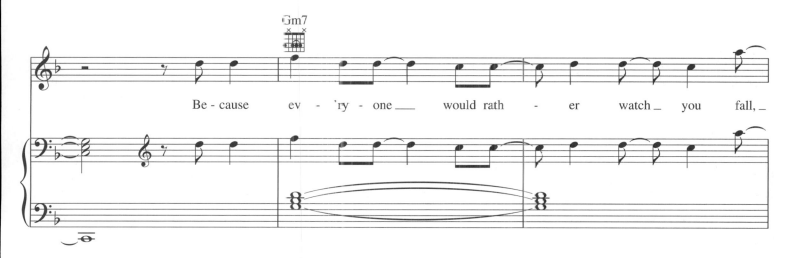

Be - cause ev - 'ry - one __ would rath - er watch __ you fall, __

__ and we all are, yeah, and we

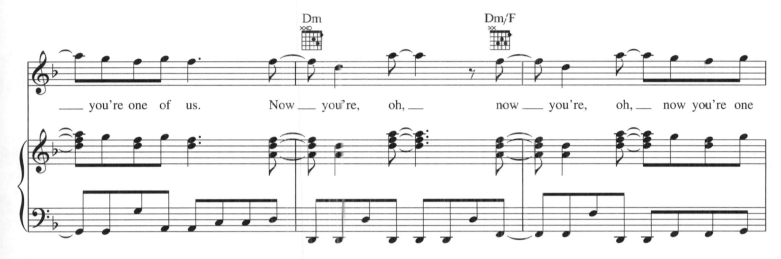

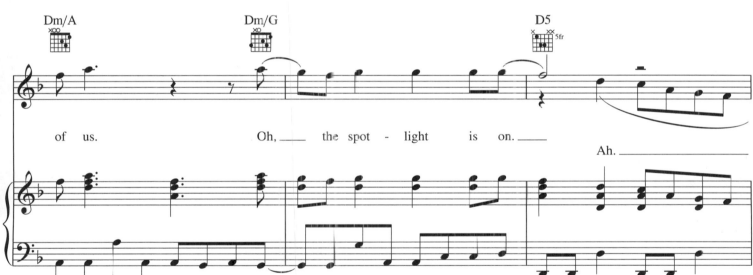

GO ALL THE WAY
(Into the Twilight)

Words and Music by ATTICUS ROSS,
PERRY FARRELL, ETTY LAU FARRELL
and CARL RESTIVO

With drive

Hap-py day, hap-py day, hap-py day, we're go-

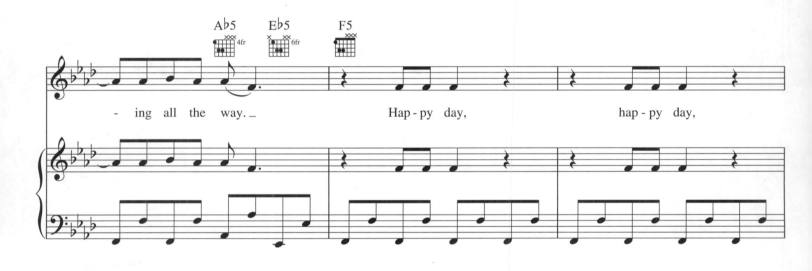

-ing all the way. _ Hap-py day, hap-py day,

hap-py day, we're go - ing all the way, _ we're go - ing all the way, _ we're go-

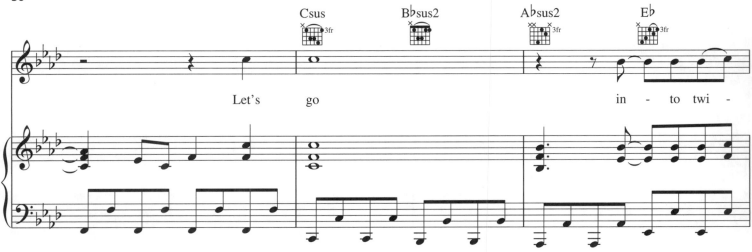

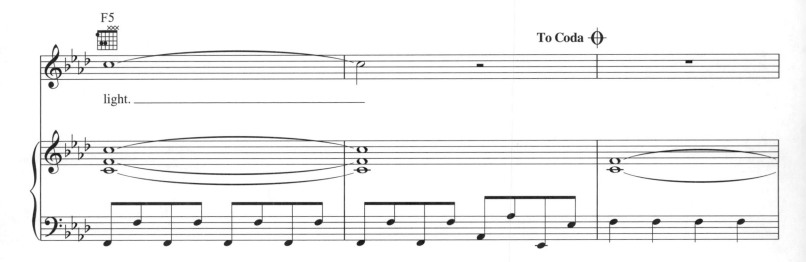

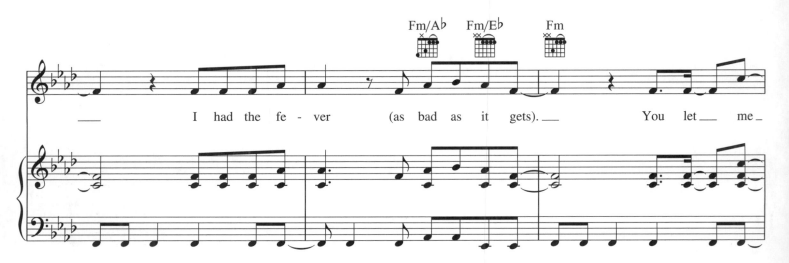

see ___ (as much in ___ my eyes), ___ it was ___ so ___

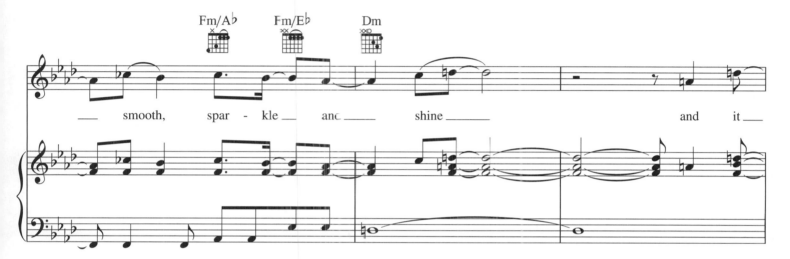

___ smooth, spar - kle ___ and ___ shine ___ and it ___

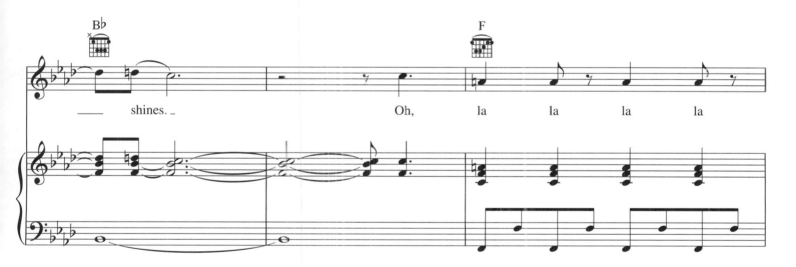

___ shines. _ Oh, la la la la la

D.S. al Coda

la la la la la la la la la la la la. To - night ___

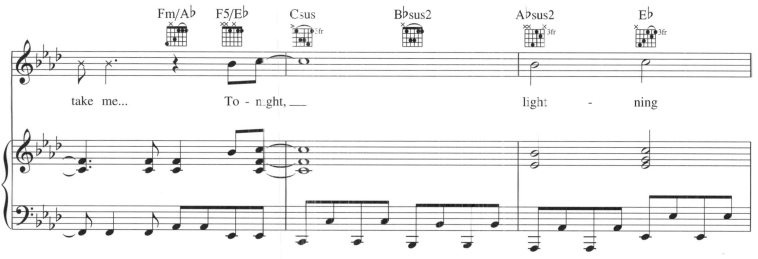

take me...   To - night, ___   light - ning

strikes. ___   Let's   go

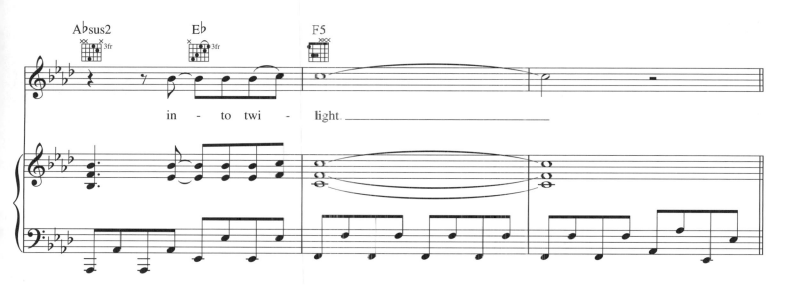

in - to twi - light. _____

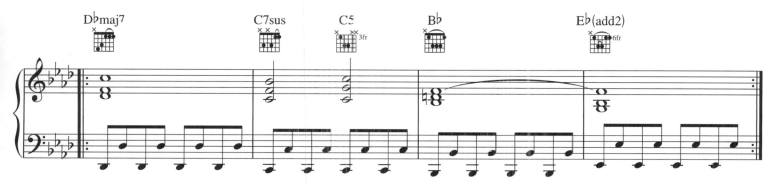

You are a - way with me, no oth - er way.

You are a - way with me, no oth - er way.

You are a - way with me, no oth - er way.

You are a - way with me, no oth - er way.

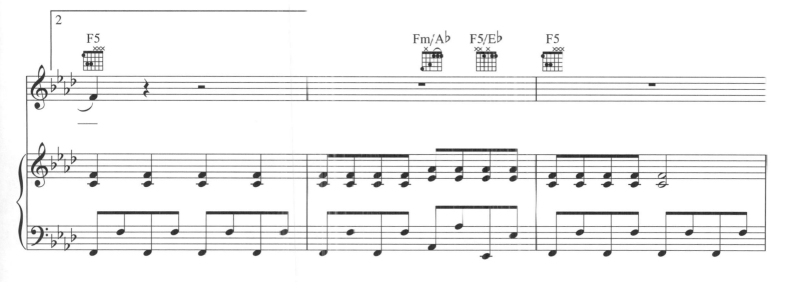

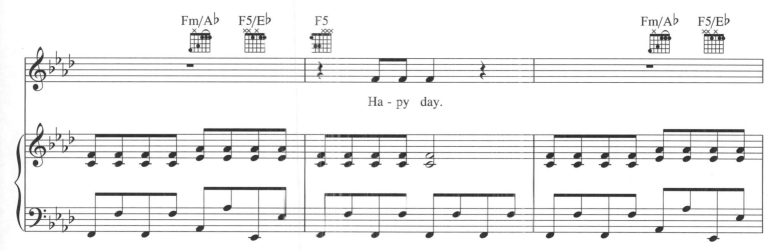

TREMBLE FOR MY BELOVED

Words and Music by
ED ROLAND

Pop Rock

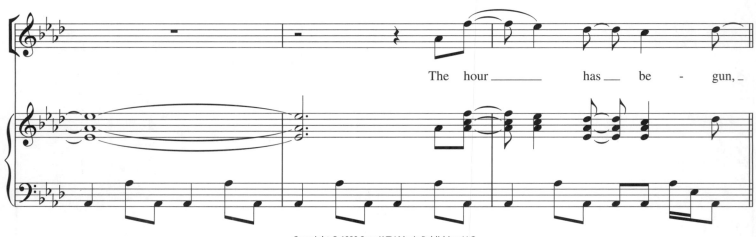

The hour _____ has ___ be - gun, ___

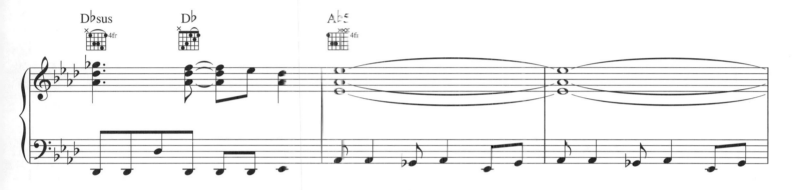

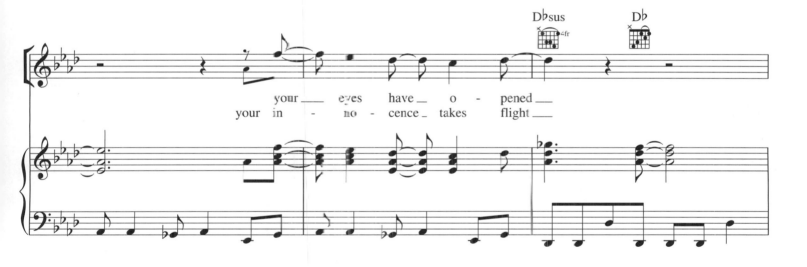

your ___ eyes have o - pened ___
your in - no - cence ___ takes flight ___

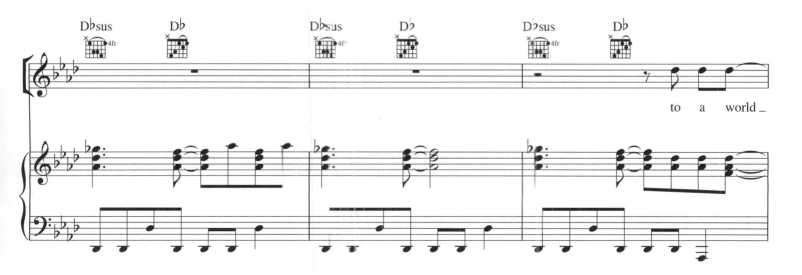

to a world ___

44

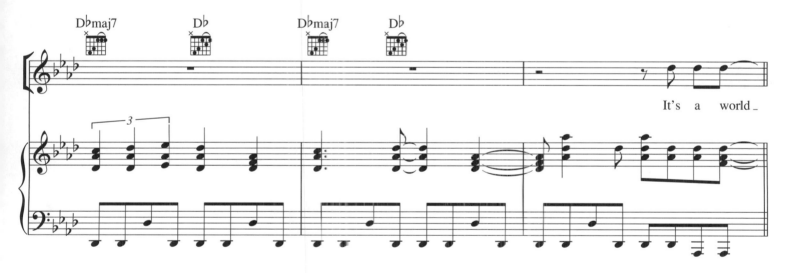

It's a world

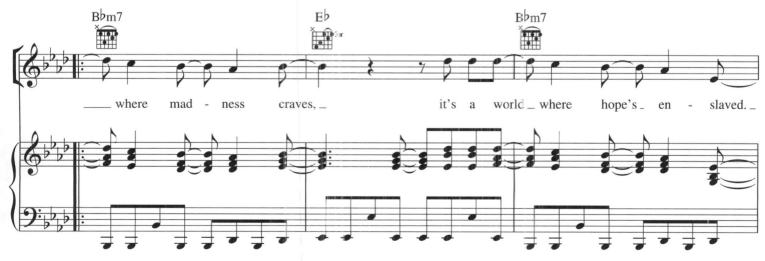

_____ where mad - ness craves, _ it's a world _ where hope's _ en - slaved. _

For I trem - ble for __ my love, __ al -
Yeah, I trem - ble for __ you, love, __ al -

ways.

It's a world __ ways.

I CAUGHT MYSELF

Words and Music by HAYLEY WILLIAMS
and JOSH FARRO

Alternative Rock

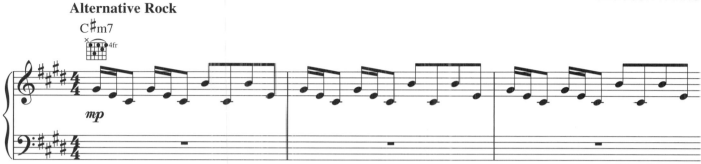

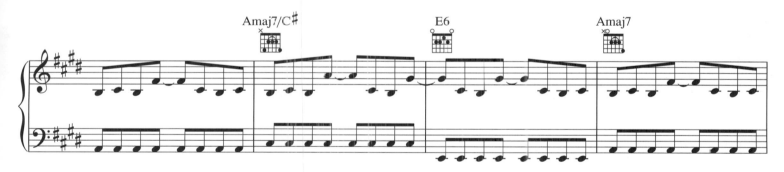

Down to you, you're push-ing _ and pull-ing _ me down to you. But

I don't _ know what I... _ Now when I caught _ my-self, I had to stop my-self,

I'm say-ing some-thing _ that I should have nev-er thought. Now when I caught _ my-self,

I had to stop my-self from say-ing some-thing _ that I should have nev-er thought of

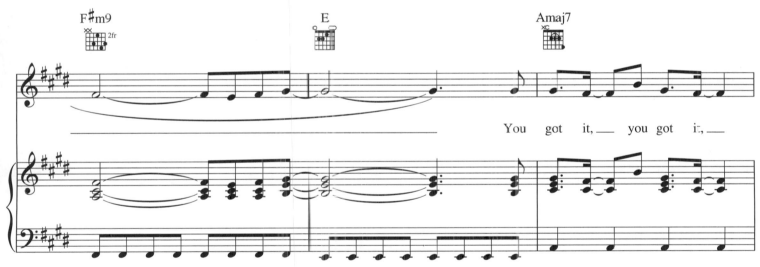

hate this, __ I hate this; __ you're not __ the one I __ be - lieve in, ___ with

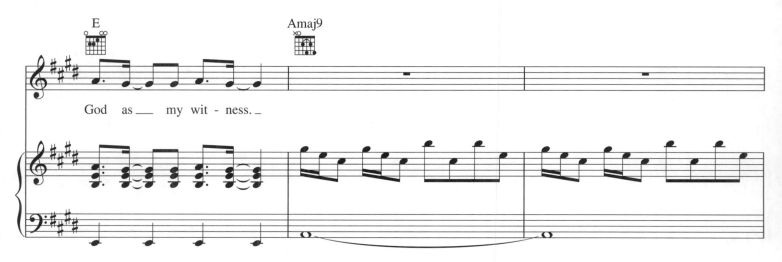

God as __ my wit - ness. __

D.S. al Coda

CODA

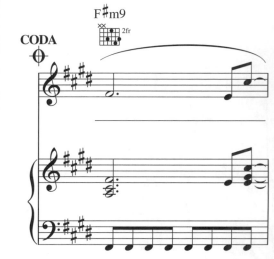

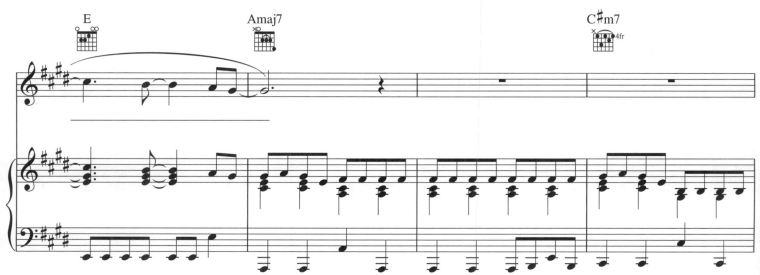

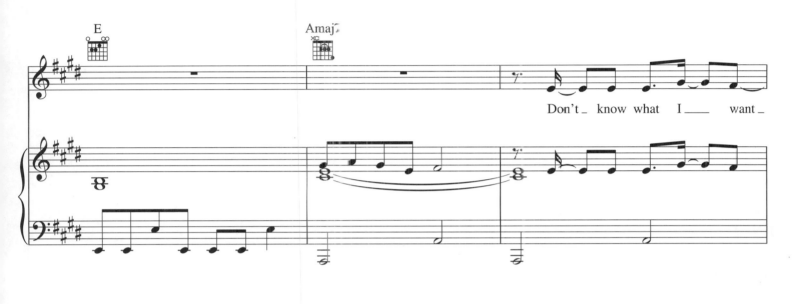

Don't _ know what I _ want _

but I know it's not _ you. _ Keep

push - ing _ and pull - ing _ me down, _ but I know in _ my heart it's _ not _

you.

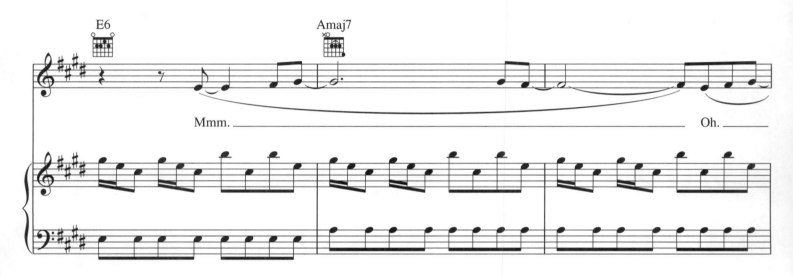

Mmm. _____ Oh. ___

Now when I caught my - self,

I had to stop my - self   from say - ing some - thing __ that   I should have nev - er thought.

EYES ON FIRE

Words and Music by TOBIAS WILNER BERTRAM (KODA)
and KRISTINE STUBBE TEGLBAERG (KODA)

Moderate Rock

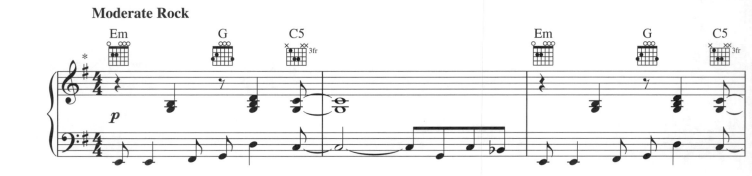

Ha _ ha _ ha _ ha _

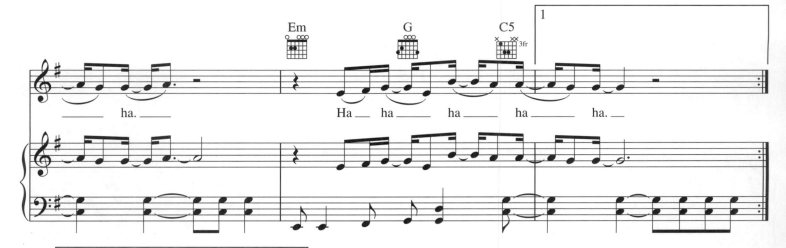

ha. _ Ha _ ha _ ha _ ha _ ha. _

ha. _ I'll seek you _ out, slay you a-live, _
tak-ing it slow, feed-ing my flame, _

* Recorded a half step lower.

one more word and you won't sur - vive. _____ And
shuf - fl - ing the cards of ____ your ___ game. ____ And

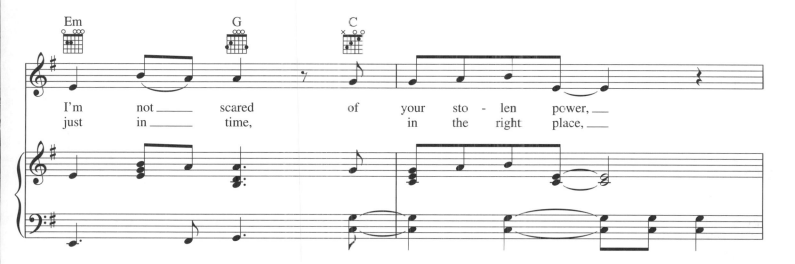

I'm not _____ scared of your sto - len power, ___
just in _____ time, in the right place, ____

see right through you an - y - how. _____ I won't
Sud - den - ly I will play my ___ ace. _____

soothe your pain, ___ I won't ease your strain. __

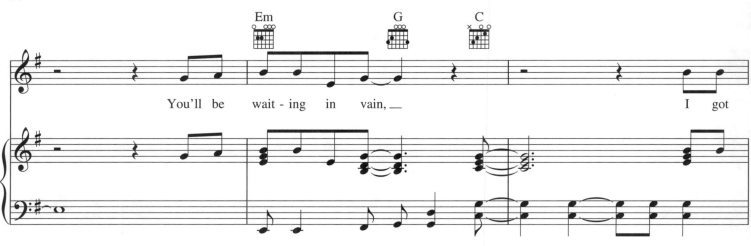

You'll be wait-ing in vain, ___ I got

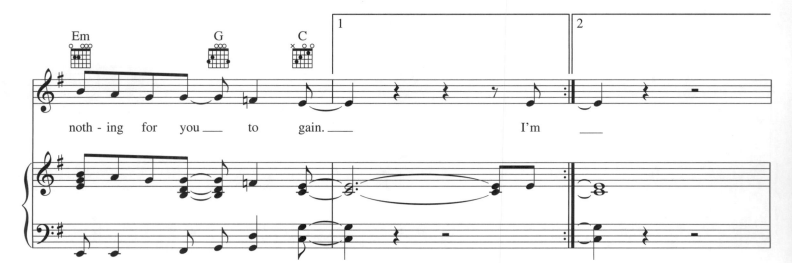

noth-ing for you ___ to gain. ___ I'm ___

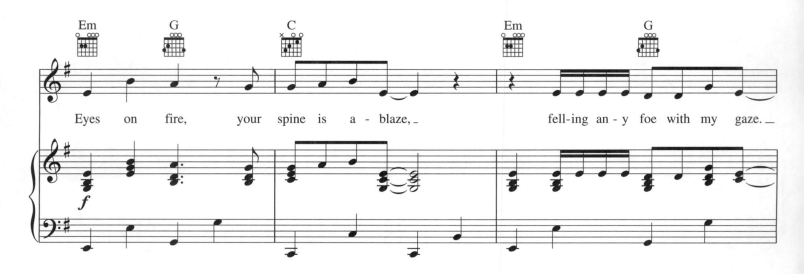

Eyes on fire, your spine is a-blaze, ___ fell-ing an-y foe with my gaze. ___

___ And just in ___ time, in the right place, ___

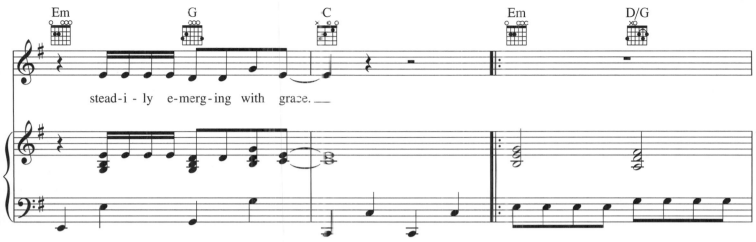

steadily e-merg-ing with grace.

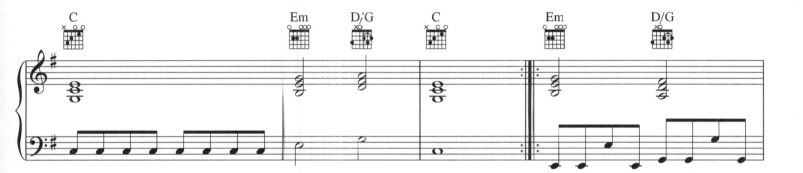

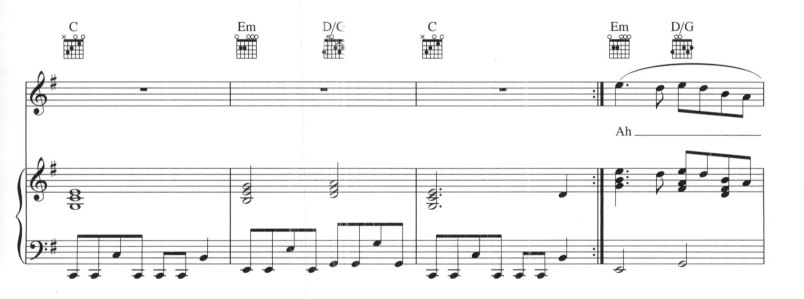

Ah

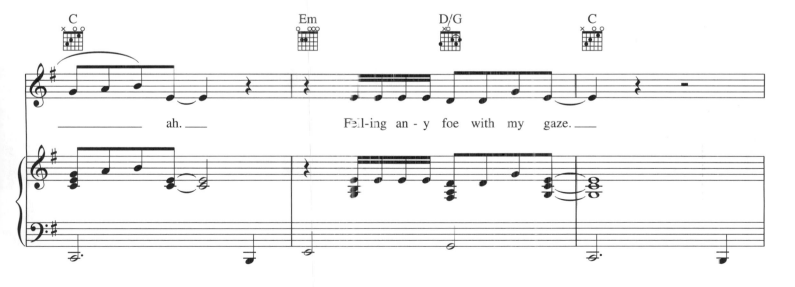

ah. Fell-ing an-y foe with my gaze.

NEVER THINK

Words and Music by SAM BRADLEY
and ROBERT PATTINSON

With freedom

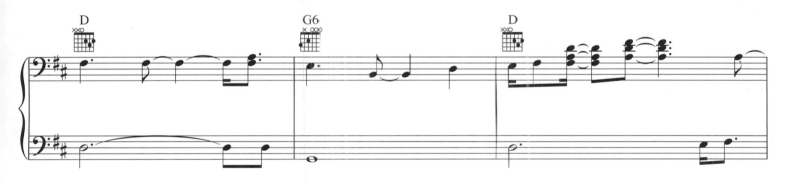

Should nev-er think ____ what's in your _

heart, _____ what's in our _____ home _____

so I won't. _

You'll learn to hate _____ me, _____ but still

call me ba - by, _____ oh, _____ love, _____ so call me by _

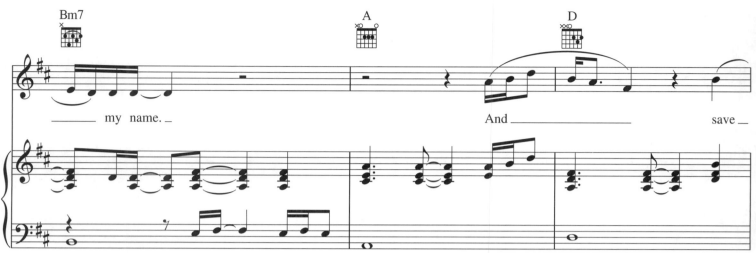

_____ my name. _____ And _____ save _____

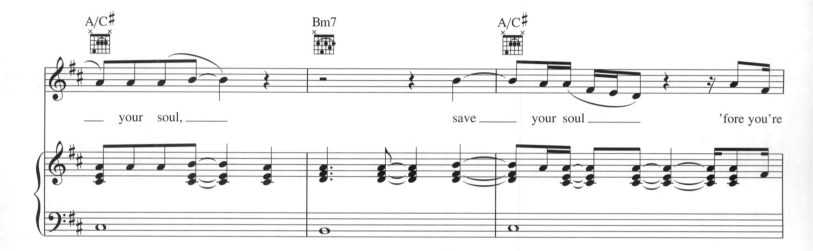

_____ your soul, _____ save _____ your soul _____ 'fore you're

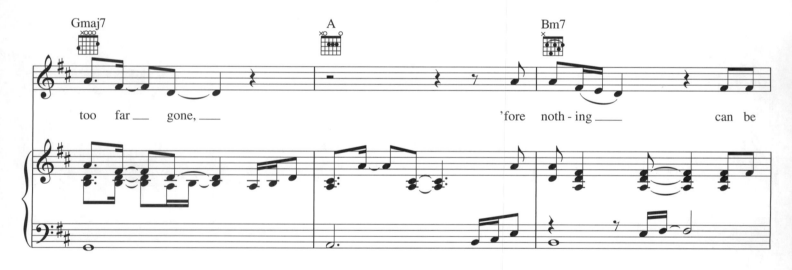

too far _____ gone, _____ 'fore noth - ing _____ can be

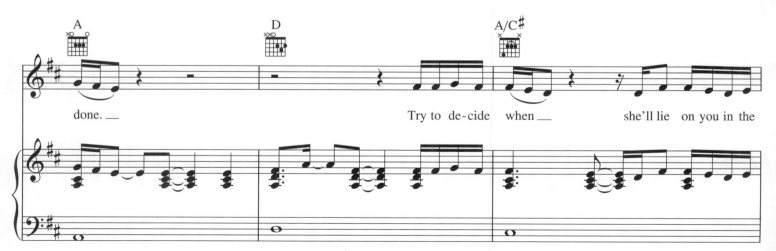

done. _____ Try to de - cide when _____ she'll lie on you in the

end. _____ Ain't got no fight in me in this whole _ damn world, tell you you

hold off, _____ you choose to

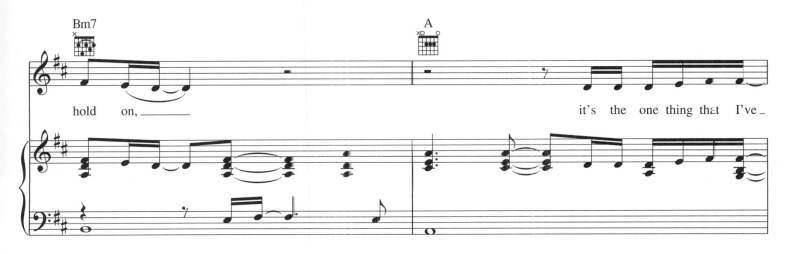

hold on, _____ it's the one thing that I've _

_ known. _ Once I put my _ coat on, com-ing out

in this all _____ wrong. _____ She's stand-ing out - side hold-ing me, _ say-ing,

"Oh, please, _ I'm in love, _____ I'm in love." _____

_ Girl, _____ save your

soul, _____ go on, save your soul _____ be - fore _

you're too far gone, and be-fore noth-ing _____ can

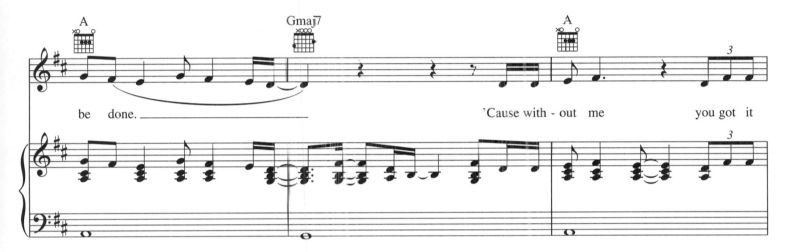

be done. _____ 'Cause with-out me you got it

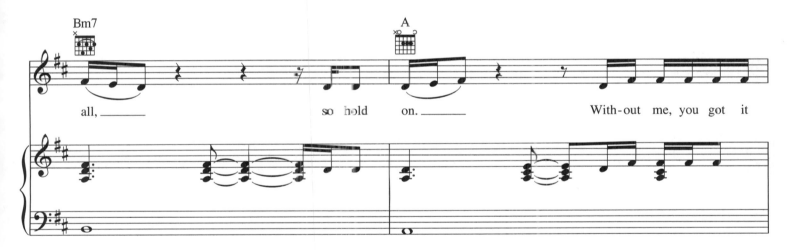

all, _____ so hold on. _____ With-out me, you got it

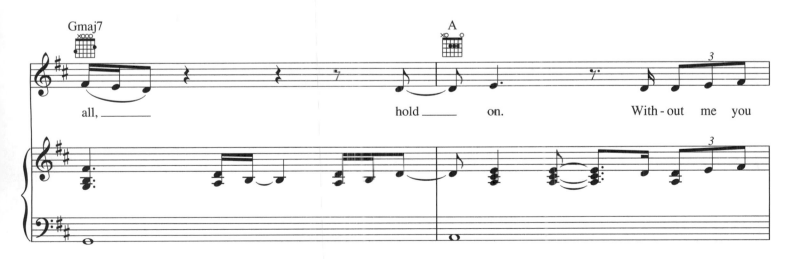

all, _____ hold ____ on. With-out me you

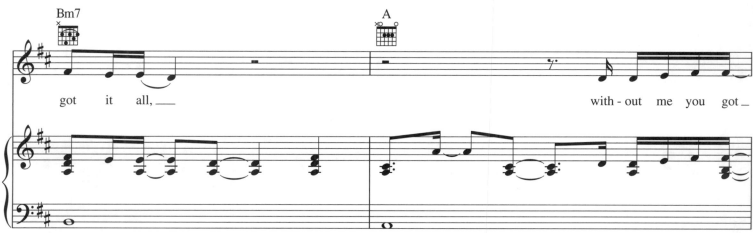

BELLA'S LULLABY

Composed by CARTER BURWELL
(for Christine)

Moderately

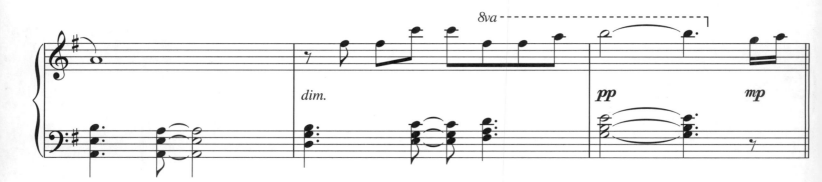

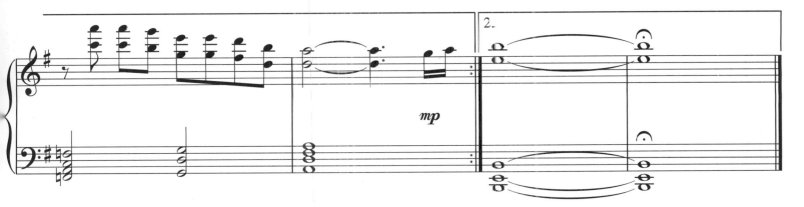